# KRONOSAURUS

## AND OTHER SEA CREATURES

# Prehistoric World

# KRONOSAURUS

## AND OTHER SEA CREATURES

VIRGINIA SCHOMP

**BENCHMARK BOOKS**

MARSHALL CAVENDISH
NEW YORK

DINOSAURS AND MANY OTHER PREHISTORIC CREATURES LIVED MILLIONS OF YEARS AGO. EVERYTHING WE KNOW ABOUT THEM—HOW THEY LOOKED, WALKED, ATE, FOUGHT, MATED, AND RAISED THEIR YOUNG—COMES FROM EDUCATED GUESSES BY THE SCIENTISTS WHO DISCOVER AND STUDY FOSSILS. THE INFORMATION IN THIS BOOK IS BASED ON WHAT MOST SCIENTISTS BELIEVE RIGHT NOW. TOMORROW OR NEXT WEEK OR NEXT YEAR, NEW DISCOVERIES COULD LEAD TO NEW IDEAS. SO KEEP YOUR EYES AND EARS OPEN FOR NEWS FLASHES FROM THE PREHISTORIC WORLD!

Benchmark Books
Marshall Cavendish
99 White Plains Road
Tarrytown, New York 10591-9001
www.marshallcavendish.com

© Marshall Cavendish Corporation 2004

Library of Congress Cataloging-in-Publication Data

Schomp, Virginia.
  Kronosaurus and other sea creatures / Virginia Schomp.
      v. cm. — (Prehistoric world)
Includes bibliographical references and index.
Contents: Monsters of the Deep — Time line: the age of dinosaurs —
Plesiosaurs and pliosaurs — Dangerous waters — Map: the early Cretaceous
world — Rulers of the deep — End of the sea monsters.
  ISBN 0-7614-1543-2
1.  Kronosaurus—Juvenile literature. 2.  Marine animals, Fossil—
Juvenile literature. [1. Kronosaurus. 2. Dinosaurs. 3. Marine
 animals, Fossil.]  I. Title. II. Series:  Schomp, Virginia.
Prehistoric world.
QE862.P4S36 2004                567.9'37—dc21                2003002012

Front cover: *Kronosaurus*          Back cover: *Proganochelys*          Pages 2–3: Ichthyosaurs

Photo Credits:

Cover illustration: Marshall Cavendish Corporation

The illustrations and photographs in this book are used by permission and through the courtesy of:
*Marshall Cavendish Corporation:* 2–3, 9, 10, 12, 14–15, 16, 18, 22, 23, 24, back cover. *The Natural History
Museum, London:* 11, 20; John Sibbick, 19; Orbis, 8, 21, 25.

Map and Reptile Family Tree by Robert Romagnoli

Printed in China

1 3 5 6 4 2

For Kayleigh and Timothy Bigness

# Contents

# MONSTERS OF THE DEEP

The earth, millions of years ago. Giant dinosaurs rule the land. In the seas, there are animals just as big, strange, and terrifying. Some look like oversize crocodiles. Some have long necks, small heads, and sharp pinlike teeth. There are even mean-looking monsters as massive as modern-day whales. Huge jaws and teeth like daggers make these giant creatures the most fearsome hunters in the sea.

Where did all these spectacular creatures come from? To answer that question, we must take a closer look at life in the prehistoric world.

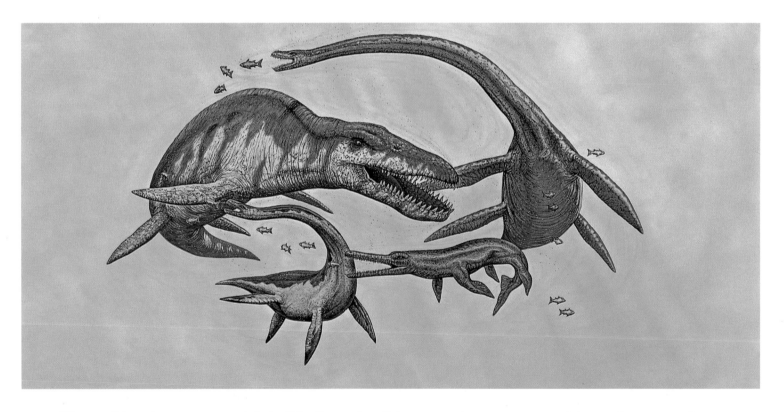

*The prehistoric seas were rich in life, from tiny fish to massive meat-eaters bigger than even the largest dinosaur.*

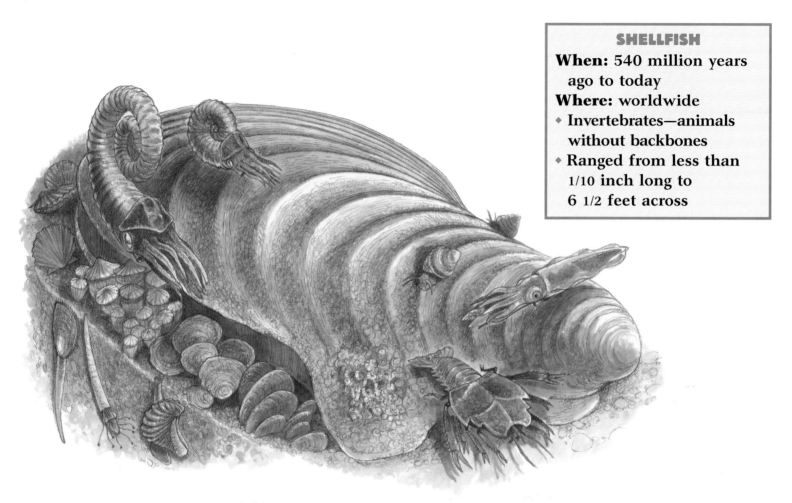

*Some kinds of shellfish appeared long before the Age of Dinosaurs and still exist today.*

## LIFE IN ANCIENT SEAS

Scientists tell us that life on earth began in the sea. Around four billion years ago, the first microscopic sea animals appeared. Then, around 600 million years ago, many kinds of larger life-forms began to develop. There were shellfish with long tentacles and wormlike creatures with big bulging eyes. There were predators with claws, spikes, and stingers.

In time, fish swam the seas. Early fish had no jaws, just a round mouth for sucking in tiny bits of food. These weird-looking creatures were the first vertebrates—animals with a backbone.

About 400 million years ago, some vertebrates crawled from the sea to try life on land. These were amphibians—animals that live partly on land, partly in the water.

**FISH**

**When:** 520 million years ago to today

**Where:** worldwide

♦ Vertebrates—animals with backbones

♦ More than 24,000 kinds today

*Early fish evolved—or slowly developed—to resemble the fish we are familiar with today. These are* Lepidotes, *a kind of freshwater fish that lived more than 100 million years ago.*

*Amphibians developed from fish that left the water, probably to avoid predators and to hunt insects on land. This* Paracyclotosaurus *was a large amphibian that lived early in the Age of Dinosaurs.*

Placodus *(top) was an early placodont with bony knobs along the spine for protection from predators.*
*Later placodonts like* Psephoderma *(bottom) had turtlelike shells.*

It took another 200 million years for full-time land dwellers called reptiles to make their appearance. Early reptiles looked a lot like amphibians, but they had scaly skin that did not dry out away from the water. Over the centuries, reptiles developed into many shapes and sizes, from tiny lizards to giant dinosaurs like *Tyrannosaurus*.

While the dinosaurs ruled the land, some reptiles returned to the sea. There they took many amazing, sometimes scary forms. Nothosaurs had long jaws with sharp teeth. Placodonts looked a lot like crocodiles with turtle shells. But the biggest and meanest-looking sea monsters were the plesiosaurs.

## The Age of Dinosaurs

*Large meat-eating reptiles ruled the seas while the dinosaurs walked the earth. These ancient creatures lived during the long span of time called the Mesozoic era, or the Age of Dinosaurs.*

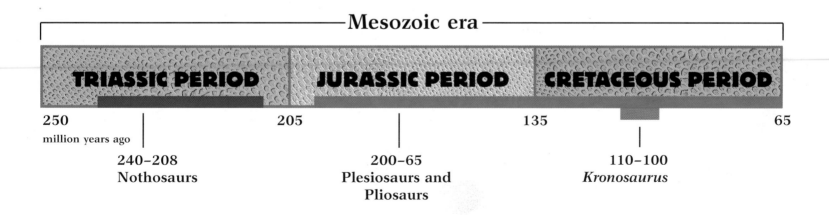

# PLESIOSAURS AND PLIOSAURS

As long as a moving van. Teeth bigger than bananas. *Kronosaurus* must have been every sea creature's worst nightmare. This giant predator belonged to the group of sea reptiles called plesiosaurs. On page 26, you can see how scientists fit the plesiosaurs into the reptile family tree.

There were two kinds of plesiosaurs. One group had small heads and very long necks. The other group had large heads and short necks. Short-necked plesiosaurs are also called pliosaurs. During the Age of Dinosaurs, pliosaurs were the most fearsome predators in the sea.

Kronosaurus *was the "Jaws" of the prehistoric world. The giant pliosaur is swimming with its cousin*
Cryptocleidus, *a medium-sized long-necked plesiosaur from Europe.*

*Kronosaurus* was one of the largest-known pliosaurs. It may have measured thirty to forty feet long. One-third of its length was its long flat head. *Kronosaurus* had a bigger head than *Tyrannosaurus*. Its jaws had the biting power of a killer whale, and its sharp teeth could rip apart even the largest, fiercest shark.

**SHARKS**
**When:** 430 million years ago to today
**Where:** worldwide
• Among the earliest vertebrates with jaws and bony teeth
• Ranged from 6 inches to 50 feet long

*Sharks are a kind of fish with skeletons made of cartilage—the flexible material in your nose and outer ear—instead of bone. Many early sharks were powerful predators, but they were no match for the giant pliosaurs.*

# DANGEROUS WATERS

The shape of the oceans and continents is always changing. About 250 million years ago, when the first large meat-eating reptiles swam in the sea, all the earth's lands were joined in a single continent surrounded by water. During the Age of Dinosaurs, that supercontinent broke into pieces. The landmasses slowly drifted apart and water flowed into the gaps. New oceans formed, and shallow seas covered many low-lying areas that today are dry land.

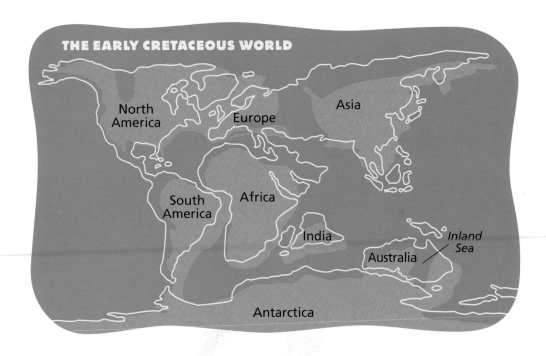

*During the Cretaceous period, the continents and oceans began to take their modern shape. The yellow outlines on this map show the shape of the continents today; the green shading shows their position around 100 million years ago, in the days of* Kronosaurus.

# HUNTERS AND HUNTED

Let's take a trip back in time 100 million years, to the world of *Kronosaurus.* A vast shallow sea covers much of Australia. The warm waters are filled with life. There are silvery schools of fish and many small ammonoids and belemnoids. All these swimmers are hunting for

**AMMONOIDS**
(AM-uh-noids)
**When:** 375–65 million years ago
**Where:** worldwide
◆ Soft-bodied animals with coiled or straight shells
◆ Ranged from 1/2 inch to 6 feet long

**BELEMNOIDS**
(BELL-um-noids)
**When:** 205–65 million years ago
**Where:** worldwide
◆ Long soft bodies with many tentacles
◆ Ranged from 4 inches to 6 1/2 feet long

*Curly-shelled ammonoids and squidlike belemnoids lived on a diet of small sea creatures. They were also an abundant source of food for larger sea reptiles.*

*These ichthyosaurs look like dolphins, but the two kinds of animals are not related. The most important difference: dolphins are mammals; ichthyosaurs were reptiles.*

breakfast—and trying to avoid becoming lunch for some larger predator.

Watch out! A sharp-toothed shark moves closer. Cruising nearby is a group of ichthyosaurs. These fish-eating reptiles look a lot like today's dolphins. Unlike dolphins, though, they move their tails from side to side instead of up and down to zoom through the water.

*This remarkable fossil was found in southern Germany. It shows the skeletons of three unborn baby ichthyosaurs inside their mother's body and a fourth baby that has just been born.*

## MARY ANNING AND THE SEA REPTILES

An eleven-year-old girl named Mary Anning discovered the first ichthyosaur skeleton. Mary lived in England in the early 1800s. She and her brother helped support their family by selling fossils that they collected by the sea. One day, they found the skeleton of a huge ichthyosaur in the wall of a cliff. Years later, Mary also found the first whole skeleton of long-necked *Plesiosaurus*. Mary's discoveries made her famous. In fact, you have probably heard of her. She is the girl who inspired the tongue twister "She sells seashells down by the seashore."

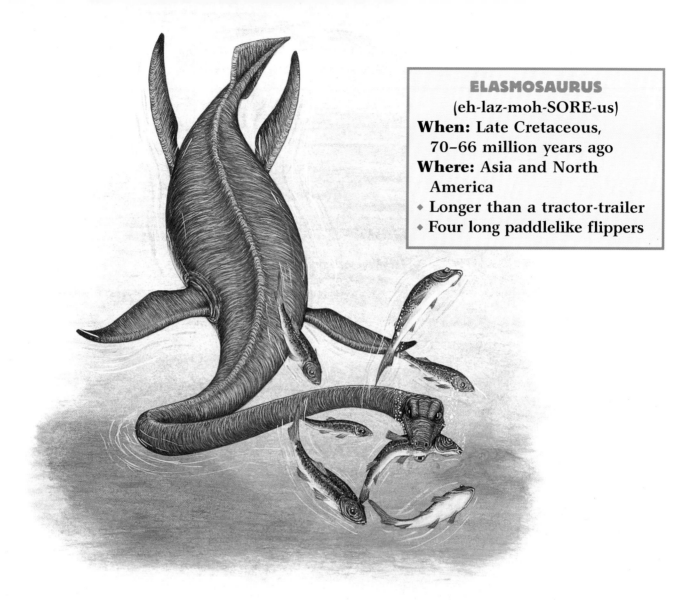

**ELASMOSAURUS**
(eh-laz-moh-SORE-us)
**When:** Late Cretaceous,
70–66 million years ago
**Where:** Asia and North
America
* Longer than a tractor-trailer
* Four long paddlelike flippers

*More than half of* Elasmosaurus's *long body was neck. This long-necked plesiosaur lived about thirty million years after* Kronosaurus.

Next we spot a *Woolungosaurus*. This long-necked plesiosaur catches fish with a quick flick of its snakelike neck.

An even deadlier hunter rules this undersea world. And when *Kronosaurus* flashes its foot-long fangs, we might decide it is time to leave these dangerous waters.

# RULERS OF THE DEEP

What made *Kronosaurus* and its short-necked cousins such successful hunters? Partly it was their long paddlelike arms and legs. The giant pliosaurs may have beat their paddles up and down like wings to "fly" swiftly through the water. Sleek, streamlined bodies made them especially fast. Chasing a slippery fish, they could use just one paddle for quick turns or all four for a burst of speed.

**MOSASAURS**
(MOH-zuh-sores)
**When:** Late Cretaceous,
75–65 million years ago
**Where:** North America, Europe,
North Africa, New Zealand
◆ Eel-like predators with long
jaws and sharp curved teeth
◆ Ranged from 7 to 30 feet long

*The mosasaurs were the last group of giant sea reptiles to appear. Some of these monstrous meat-eaters were larger than a great white shark.*

*Even a giant sea turtle could become a snack for a ferocious pliosaur. This is* Proganochelys, *an early turtle that could not pull its head or legs into its shell.*

Size was another advantage. The long-necked and short-necked plesiosaurs were the biggest creatures in the sea. That put just about anything that moved on the menu. *Kronosaurus* probably used the rounded teeth at the back of its jaws to crunch ammonoids and other hard-shelled meals. The sharper teeth in the front carved up large fish, turtles, ichthyosaurs, and other plesiosaurs. Sometimes this mega-monster may even have attacked careless dinosaurs that strayed too near the water.

# END OF THE SEA MONSTERS

The dinosaurs died out about 65 million years ago. So did the plesiosaurs and most other large reptiles on land and in the sea. But some animals lived on, including lizards, snakes, small turtles and crocodiles, birds, and small furry mammals.

The oceans are still filled with life. There are fish, shellfish, and sea mammals like dolphins and whales. But the ancient sea monsters are gone.

Or are they?

**CROCODILES**
**When:** 200 million years ago to today
**Where:** worldwide
◆ **Lived on land, in freshwater, and in the sea**
◆ **Ranged from 8 inches to 50 feet long**

*The ancient crocodile* Deinosuchus *surprises a young meat-eating dinosaur. Scientists are not certain why the dinosaurs and many other creatures became extinct while crocodiles and some other animals survived.*

*This toothy sea dweller is a coelacanth, a kind of fish that developed about 400 million years ago. Scientists once believed that the coelacanths had all died out, but now they know that small groups still live in the Indian Ocean.*

In 1938, fishermen off the coast of Africa found an odd-looking sharp-toothed fish in their nets. It was a coelacanth—a kind of fish that scientists thought had been extinct for millions of years. This "living fossil" remained unknown for so long because it lives deep in the ocean. Who knows what other mysteries of the prehistoric world still lie hidden beneath the waves?

# Reptile Family Tree

**ORDER**

An order is a large group of animals. Plesiosaurs and pliosaurs belong to the same order.

**SUPERFAMILY**

Plesiosaurs had long necks and small heads. Pliosaurs had short necks and large heads.

**FAMILY**

A family includes one or more types of closely related animals.

**GENUS**

Every animal has a two-word name. The first word tells us what genus, or type, of animal it is. The genus plus the second word are its species—the group of very similar animals it belongs to. (For example, *Kronosaurus queenslandicus* is one species of *Kronosaurus*.)

Scientists often disagree about how the ancient reptiles should be classified, or organized into groups according to features shared. This chart shows one possible grouping of some of the prehistoric sea creatures described in this book.

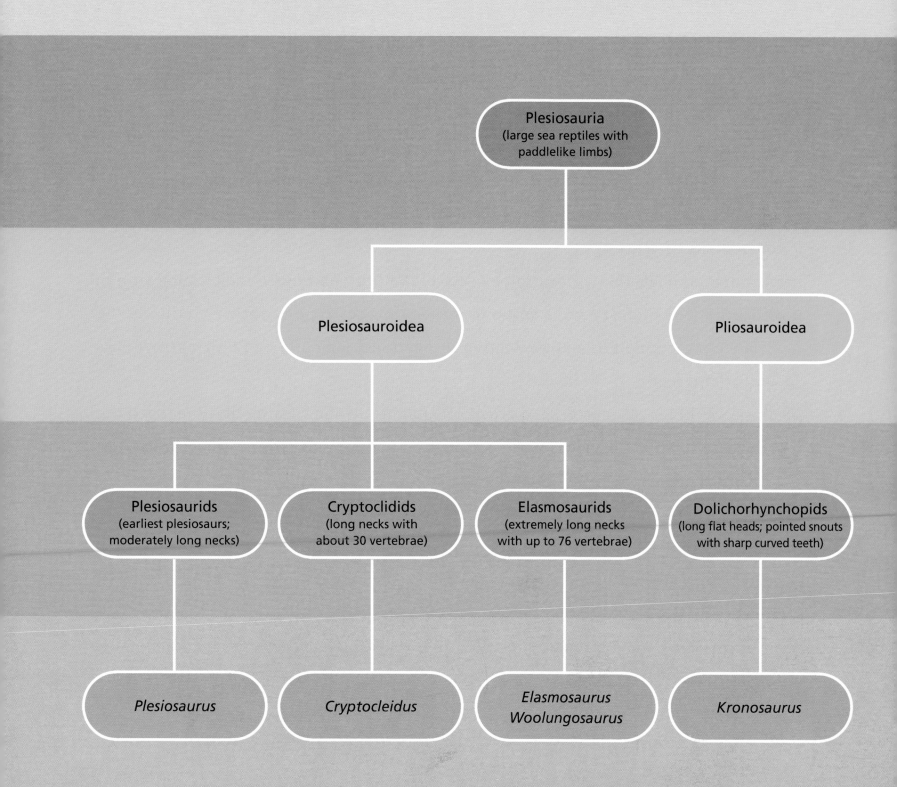

Plesiosauria
(large sea reptiles with paddlelike limbs)

Plesiosauroidea

Pliosauroidea

Plesiosaurids
(earliest plesiosaurs; moderately long necks)

Cryptoclidids
(long necks with about 30 vertebrae)

Elasmosaurids
(extremely long necks with up to 76 vertebrae)

Dolichorhynchopids
(long flat heads; pointed snouts with sharp curved teeth)

*Plesiosaurus*

*Cryptocleidus*

*Elasmosaurus*
*Woolungosaurus*

*Kronosaurus*

# Glossary

**amphibians** (am-FIH-bee-inz):  vertebrate animals that live part of the time on land, part in the water; frogs, toads, and salamanders are modern amphibians

**Cretaceous** (krih-TAY-shus) **period:**  the time period from about 135 million to 65 million years ago, during which *Kronosaurus* and many other plesiosaurs lived

**extinct:**  no longer existing; an animal is extinct when every one of its kind has died

**fossils:**  the hardened remains or traces of animals or plants that lived many thousands or millions of years ago

**mammals:**  animals that are warm-blooded, breathe air, and nurse their young with milk

**nothosaurs** (NO-thoh-sores):  a group of meat-eating sea reptiles that lived during the Triassic period; nothosaurs grew up to thirteen feet long and had long narrow jaws with sharp teeth

**plesiosaurs** (PLEE-zee-oh-sores):  a group of large meat-eating sea reptiles that lived during the Jurassic and Cretaceous periods; one kind had long necks and small heads, and the other had short necks and large heads

**pliosaurs** (PLIE-oh-sores):  short-necked plesiosaurs

**predators:**  animals that hunt and kill other animals for food

**reptiles:**  animals that have scaly skin and, in most cases, lay eggs; crocodiles, turtles, dinosaurs, and plesiosaurs are reptiles

**vertebrates:**  animals with a backbone; fish, amphibians, reptiles, birds, and mammals are vertebrates

# Find Out More

## BOOKS

Atkins, Jeannine. *Mary Anning and the Sea Dragon.* New York: Farrar, Straus, Giroux, 1999.

*The Humongous Book of Dinosaurs.* New York: Stewart, Tabori, and Chang, 1997.

Johnston, Marianne. *Sea Turtles Past and Present.* New York: Rosen, 2000.

Lauber, Patricia. *Living with Dinosaurs.* New York: Macmillan, 1991.

Lessem, Don. *Dinosaurs to Dodos: An Encyclopedia of Extinct Animals.* New York: Scholastic, 1999.

Marshall, Chris, ed. *Dinosaurs of the World.* 11 vols. New York: Marshall Cavendish, 1999.

Piqué, Josep. *Crocodilians: Survivors from the Dinosaur Age.* Milwaukee: Gareth Stevens, 1996.

*The Prehistoric Ocean.* Vol. 3 of *Library of the Oceans.* Danbury, CT: Grolier Educational, 1998.

# ON-LINE SOURCES*

*Oceans of Kansas Paleontology: "Fossils from the Western Interior Sea"* **at http://www.oceansofkansas.com/index.html**
This excellent website created by Mike Everhart at the Sternberg Museum of Natural History in Hays, Kansas, offers a "virtual journey" back in time to observe the many creatures that lived in the sea toward the end of the Age of Dinosaurs. Click on one of the topics in the index (for example, "About mosasaurs," "About pliosaurs," or "Plesiosaur dig") for pages full of information and giant illustrations and photos.

*Paleontological Museum* **at http://www.toyen.uio.no/palmus/galleri/index_e.html**
The Paleontological Museum at the University of Oslo, Norway, has created an easy-to-navigate website with colorful photos of its fossil exhibits. There are prehistoric fish, ammonoids, amphibians, and marine reptiles, including ichthyosaurs, nothosaurs, plesiosaurs, and pliosaurs.

*Zoom Sharks* **at http://www.enchantedlearning.com/subjects/sharks**
This colorful site from Enchanted Learning Software includes lots of easy-to-read information on sharks, including ancient extinct forms.

*Website addresses sometimes change. For more on-line sources, check with the media specialist at your local library.*

# Index

**Virginia Schomp** grew up in a quiet suburban town in northeastern New Jersey, where eight-ton duck-billed dinosaurs once roamed. In first grade she discovered that she loved books and writing, and in sixth grade she was named "class bookworm," because she always had her nose in a book. Today she is a freelance author who has written more than forty books for young readers on topics including careers, animals, ancient cultures, and modern history. Ms. Schomp lives in the Catskill Mountain region of New York with her husband, Richard, and their son, Chip.